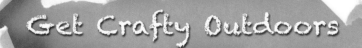

Get Crafty Outdoors

Science and Craft Projects with

INSECTS,

SPIDERS, AND OTHER MINIBEASTS

by Ruth Owen

PowerKiDS
press™

New York

Published in 2013 by The Rosen Publishing Group, Inc.
29 East 21st Street, New York, NY 10010

Produced for Rosen by Ruby Tuesday Books Ltd
Editor for Ruby Tuesday Books Ltd: Mark J. Sachner
US Editor: Sara Antill
Designer: Emma Randall
Consultant: Suzy Gazlay

Photo Credits:
Cover, 1, 4–5, 6–7, 10–11, 14 (top left), 14 (bottom), 15, 16–17, 18–19, 20, 22, 23 (right), 25, 26–27, 28, 29 (top) © Shutterstock; 8–9, 12–13, 21, 29 (bottom) © Ruby Tuesday Books Ltd; 14 (top right), 23 (left) © Wikipedia Creative Commons.

Library of Congress Cataloging-in-Publication Data

Owen, Ruth, 1967–
 Science and craft projects with insects, spiders, and other minibeasts /
by Ruth Owen.
    p. cm. — (Get crafty outdoors)
 Includes index.
 ISBN 978-1-4777-0245-1 (library binding) — ISBN 978-1-4777-0253-6 (pbk.) —
ISBN 978-1-4777-0254-3 (6-pack)
1. Ecology–Juvenile literature. 2. Nature study—Juvenile literature. 3. Insects—
Juvenile literature. 4. Spiders—Juvenile literature. 5. Handicraft—Juvenile
literature. I. Title.
 QH541.14.O89 2013
 577—dc23

                                2012030884

Manufactured in the United States of America

CPSIA Compliance Information: Batch #W13PK7: For Further Information contact Rosen Publishing, New York, New York at 1-800-237-9932

Contents

Meet Some Minibeasts

Inside this book, you will find out about some of the fascinating insects, spiders, and minibeasts that share our world. You will also get the chance to make some fun critter crafts!

Insects are tiny animals with six legs and two **antennae**. All insects have three main body parts—a head, a **thorax**, and an **abdomen**.

An insect does not have a skeleton inside its body. Instead, it has a hard outer shell, or skin, called an **exoskeleton**.

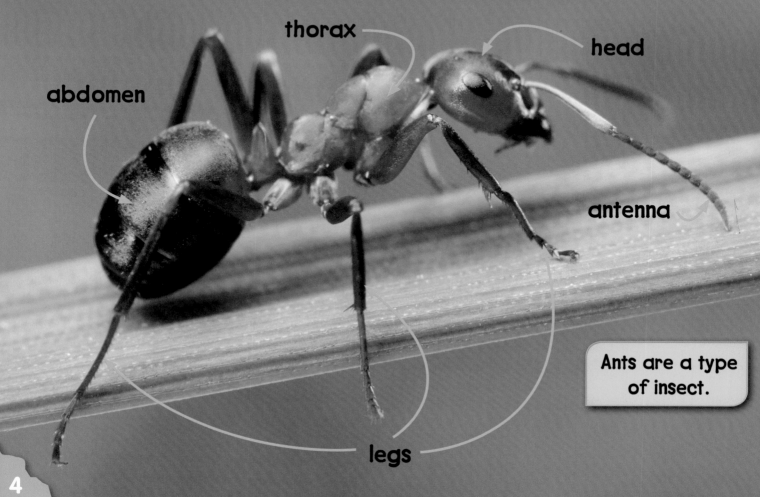

thorax

head

abdomen

antenna

legs

Ants are a type of insect.

Spiders are not insects. They belong to an animal group called **arachnids**.

A spider has two main body parts called a **cephalothorax** and an abdomen. All spiders have eight legs. They also have two **palps**, which they use for tasting food.

cephalothorax

abdomen

This is a jumping spider.

palps

legs

What Are Minibeasts?

The word "minibeast" is a fun word used to describe a very small animal. Insects, spiders, and other tiny creatures, such as snails, slugs, and earthworms, are all known as minibeasts.

earthworm

Lovely Ladybugs

Ladybugs are small, colorful insects. There are around 5,000 different types of ladybugs in the world.

Ladybugs are a type of flying insect. When they are not flying, they keep their wings tucked under two hard wing covers. When in flight, they beat their wings about 85 times per second!

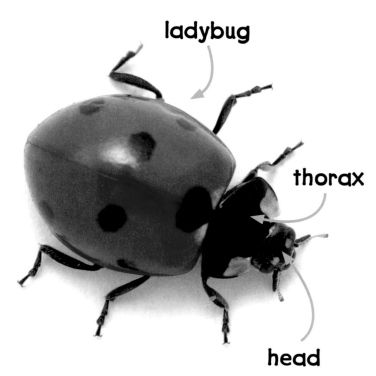

ladybug

thorax

head

wing covers

wing

abdomen

Ladybugs are **predators** that hunt and eat other small insects. Their favorite food is aphids. Ladybugs can eat up to 75 of these little creatures each day.

Aphids feed by sucking the juices out of plants. This can damage or kill a plant. Farmers and gardeners like ladybugs because they help protect plants and **crops** from aphids.

aphid

Colors for Protection

A ladybug can have red, yellow, orange, or black wing covers. A ladybug's bright color warns predators, such as birds and other insects, not to attack it. If an enemy ignores the warning, the ladybug fights back by releasing a disgusting, stinky smell from its knees.

Ladybug Dominoes

Most ladybugs have black spots on their wing covers. Some ladybugs have no spots, however. Have fun making these spotty ladybug dominoes, and then challenge a friend to a game of dominoes!

You will need:

- Cardboard
- Scissors
- Red and black paint or pens
- An adult to be your teammate and help with cutting

Get Crafty:

1 Ask an adult to help you cut the cardboard into 28 domino pieces that are 3 inches (7.6 cm) long and 1 inch (2.5 cm) wide.

2 Paint or draw two ladybugs on each domino. On page 9 you will see how many spots the ladybugs on each domino should have. Make sure your dominoes match the dominoes on page 9.

How to play dominoes

- Turn all the dominoes picture-side down.
- Each player chooses seven dominoes and keeps them hidden from the other player. The spare dominoes are left picture-side down to the side of the game.
- The player with the highest double number domino (player 1) starts by placing that domino picture-side up.
- Now player 2 places a domino that has the same number of spots, so the matching halves are touching.

- Then player 1 places a domino that matches. The players continue to take turns. Dominoes can be placed at either end of the row in a straight line or at right angles to the domino they match.

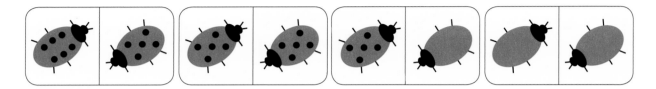

- If a player can't make a match, he or she takes a domino from the spares. That player continues to take dominoes from the spares until it's possible to make a match.
- The winner is the player who places all his or her dominoes first!

Domino patterns for drawing

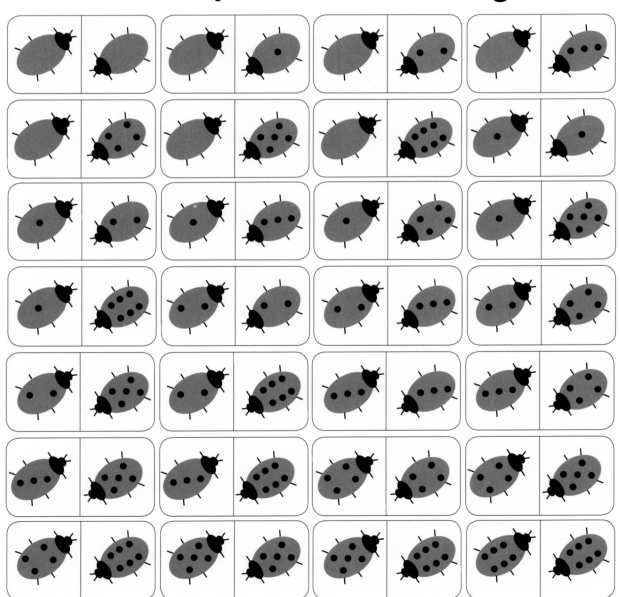

Butterflies

A butterfly is an insect with four wings. Like all insects, it has a head, a thorax, an abdomen, and six legs.

front wings

antennae

head

legs

back wing

abdomen

thorax

A butterfly has an antenna on either side of its head. It uses its two antennae to smell food. The antennae also help the butterfly to balance.

Butterflies feed on a sweet liquid called nectar that is made by flowers. To find nectar, a butterfly uses its wings to fly from flower to flower.

proboscis

proboscis

A butterfly drinks nectar using a long tongue called a proboscis. This body part is a little like a drinking straw. When the butterfly has finished drinking, it curls its proboscis up into a spiral.

Be a Butterfly Spy

In spring and summer, try to spot a butterfly visiting flowers in your backyard or at the park. While the butterfly is feeding, use a magnifying glass to look at its body. Which body parts can you see?

Make a Butterfly

Make a beautiful butterfly with finger paint handprints for wings. In the fall, you can collect dry leaves to make the butterfly's wings.

You will need:

- A large piece of thin brown cardboard
- A large piece of white cardboard
- Finger paints or 4 large, dry fall leaves
- Scissors
- 4 pipe cleaners
- Peel-and-stick wiggly eyes
- Glue and tape
- An adult to be your teammate

Get Crafty:

1 Draw a small circle, a medium-sized circle, and an oval on the brown cardboard. Ask an adult to help you cut out your shapes.

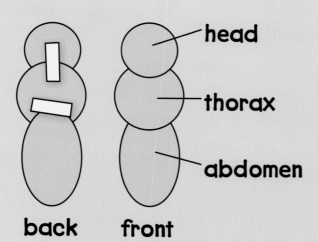

head

thorax

abdomen

back   front

2 Glue or tape your shapes together. They should overlap slightly. You've made a butterfly's head, thorax, and abdomen.

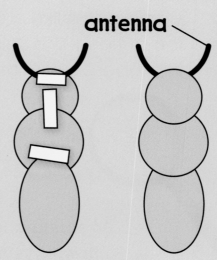

antenna

3 Bend a pipe cleaner into a U shape. Tape it behind the butterfly's head to make its antennae.

4 Tape the other three pipe cleaners behind the thorax. Now your butterfly has three pairs of legs.

5 Stick the wiggly eyes on your butterfly's face. If you are using leaves for the wings, tape them behind the butterfly's thorax to make its four wings.

6 If you are making handprint wings, ask an adult to help you pour some paint into flat containers or dishes.

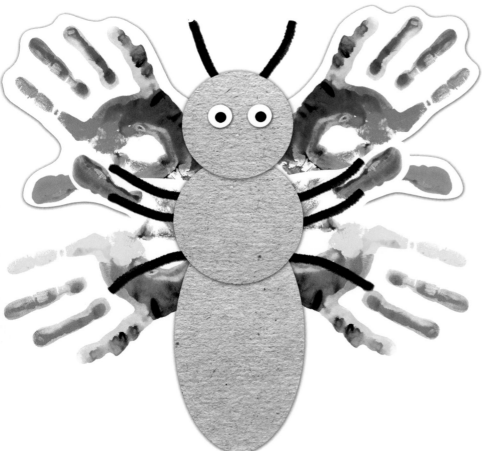

7 Make four colorful handprints on the white cardboard. Spread your fingers as wide as you can.

8 When the handprints are dry, ask an adult to help you cut them out.

9 Tape your handprints behind the butterfly's thorax to make its four wings.

Butterfly Babies

When it's time to have baby bugs, a male and female insect **mate**. Then the female insect lays eggs. All baby insects, from ladybugs to butterflies, hatch from eggs.

a monarch butterfly

butterfly egg

A female monarch butterfly lays about 400 eggs at one time. A tiny caterpillar hatches from each egg and begins to munch on plants.

Very Hungry Caterpillars

A monarch caterpillar eats a lot and grows very fast. Every few days its skin gets too tight. It splits out of its old skin, and there's a new, bigger skin underneath.

monarch caterpillar

This is a step-by-step picture of a caterpillar becoming a chrysalis.

When a monarch caterpillar is about two weeks old, it splits out of its striped skin. Now the caterpillar has become a green chrysalis. The chrysalis is inside a see-through case.

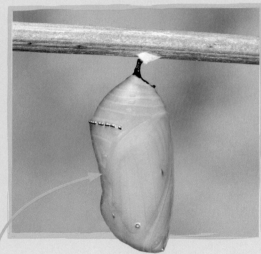

a chrysalis inside its see-through case

case

Inside the see-through case, the chrysalis starts to change. Finally, after about 10 days, the case cracks open and a brand new butterfly climbs out!

new monarch butterfly

Pebble Caterpillar Sculpture

Make a cute caterpillar sculpture from pebbles to place in your yard or on a window ledge. This colorful caterpillar will also make a great gift for a friend or family member to put in their garden.

You will need:

- Five large pebbles
- A small brush
- Warm water and soap
- Two colors of acrylic (waterproof) paints for the caterpillar's body, and colors to paint a face
- Paintbrushes
- Clear varnish (available online and from craft stores)
- An adult teammate to go pebble hunting with you

Get Crafty:

1 Go pebble hunting at the beach or at the edges of a lake or river. Ask friends, neighbors, or family members if you can look for large stones or pebbles in their gardens, too. You can also buy pebbles from garden centers.

2 Use the small brush to scrub the pebbles clean in warm water and soap. Then allow them to dry.

3 Paint three pebbles in one color, and two in another color.

4 Paint the top of each pebble first. When the top has dried, turn the pebble over and paint the bottom.

5 Paint a fun face at the end of one pebble.

6 When all the pebbles are dry, paint each one with clear varnish. This will help protect the pebbles from the weather and from becoming chipped.

7 Once the varnish is dry, your sculpture is ready to be placed outside. Because the sculpture is in several separate sections, you can choose how to position it. Perhaps it can be straight one day and wiggly the next!

Silky Spider Webs

There are about 40,000 different types of spiders in the world, but there's one amazing thing that all spiders have in common. They can make **silk inside their bodies!**

A spider makes silk inside its abdomen. It releases the silk as a thin thread from a body part called a spinneret.

spinneret

abdomen

This orb-weaver spider is wrapping a dragonfly in silk thread.

Orb-weaver spiders use their sticky, silk thread to build webs for catching insects.

The spider hides at the outer edge of its web. When an insect flies or walks into the web, it gets stuck on the threads. The spider scurries over to its **prey** and ties up its victim using more silk thread.

The spider can feed on the insect immediately, or keep it trapped for later!

Web Spotting

Orb-weaver spiders live in many parts of the world. Find out if they live near you by looking for their webs. You need to look for a web with a pattern like the one in this picture.

threads that look like the spokes on a bicycle wheel

circles of silk thread that get bigger from the center

Catch a Spider's Web

Here's a great project that uses a real-life spider web to make a beautiful picture that you can frame and hang on a wall.

You will need:

- A spider's web
- A piece of black cardboard or construction paper 12 inches by 12 inches (30 x 30 cm)
- A can of silver or glitter spray paint
- A can of hairspray
- A sheet of newspaper
- A helper

Get Crafty:

1 Look outside for a spider's web. It's worth having two or three practice tries at this project so that when you find a perfect web, you will be really good at catching it.

2 It's important that you check to be sure the spider has left the web before you start. Look carefully at the whole web to be sure the spider isn't hiding off to one side.

This web is perfect for catching!

3. Spray one side of the web with the spray paint. If the web is close to a building or plants, ask a helper to hold up a sheet of newspaper behind the web so that the paint doesn't spray through the web and damage things that are nearby.

4. Allow the web to dry for about 10 minutes.

5. Now, spray hairspray over the black cardboard. Hold the cardboard behind the web, and then gently push the cardboard against the web until the web sticks to the hairspray on the cardboard.

6. When the hairspray has dried and is no longer sticky, your silver or glitter spider's web is ready to be put into a frame.

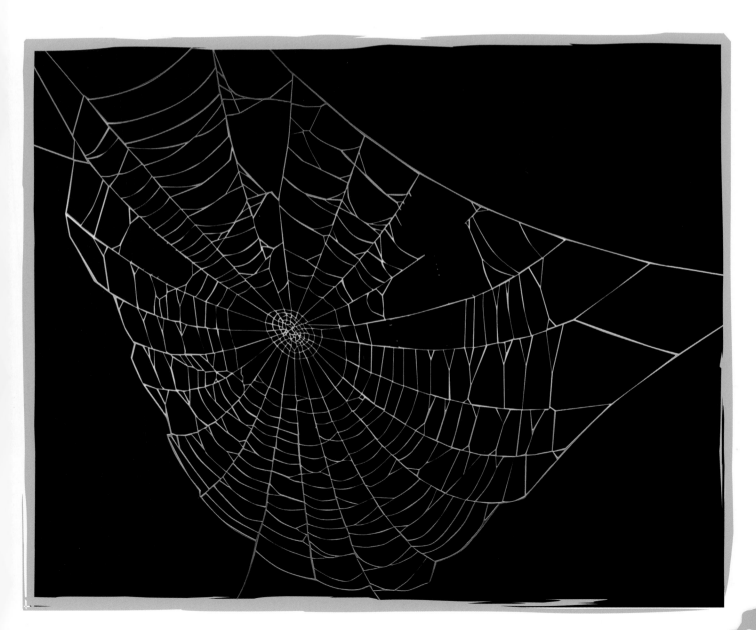

Meet a Garden Snail

A garden snail is a small animal with one giant foot and a hiding place that it carries on its back. These plant-munching minibeasts are **invertebrates**, which means they have no backbone.

This garden snail is using its large foot to move along a branch.

spiral shell

eyes

tentacle or eye stalk

head

large foot

Snails have a hard outer shell in a spiral shape. When a snail is disturbed or under attack from a predator, it can squeeze its whole body into its shell.

A snail moves along on its single, long foot. The foot oozes slime, which helps the snail slide over rough surfaces. The slime also helps the snail stick to walls. It can even stay stuck to surfaces when it is upside-down!

a snail sealed up in its shell

Keeping Cool

Garden snails like to live where it is cool and damp. If the weather gets too hot and dry, a snail will hide in its shell and seal up the entrance with slime. It may stay inside its shell for several months until the weather changes.

23

Make a Snail Racetrack

Snails sometimes move slowly, and sometimes they move fast! Make this fun snail racetrack and check out if there are any gold medal–winning minibeasts living in your neighborhood.

You will need:

- Garden snails
- A large piece of black cardboard or poster board
- White chalk
- A large mixing bowl
- A saucer
- A sheet of white paper
- Scissors
- Colored pens
- Double-sided tape
- A bucket
- A flashlight
- An audience to cheer for the snails

Get Crafty:

1. To make the racetrack, place the mixing bowl upside-down on the black cardboard and draw around it with the chalk to make a large circle.

2. Now draw around the saucer to make a small chalk circle.

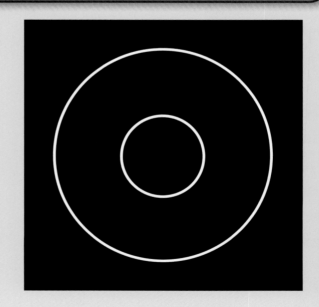

3 To make your snails' racing numbers, cut the white paper into squares about 1 inch by 1 inch (2.5 x 2.5 cm). Write a number on each square. Put a small piece of double-sided tape on the back of each numbered square.

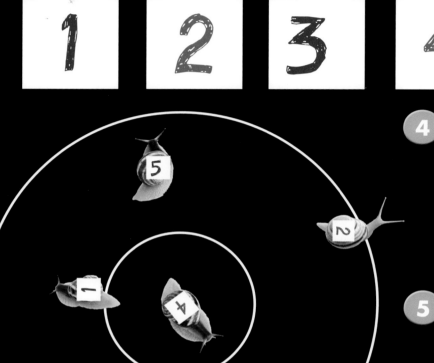

4 About one to two hours after sunset, use a flashlight to search for snails outside. Put them into the bucket. Collect two snails for each person watching, in case some of the snails won't come out of their shells.

5 Each person in the audience should choose a snail to cheer for.

6 Hold up each snail and gently press a number onto the top of its shell. Don't press on the snails when they are on a hard surface as you might squash them.

7 Dim the lights, because snails are more active in the dark. Put the racers into the center circle on the racetrack and watch them go!

8 The winner is the first snail to reach the outer circle. You will be able to see the snails' slime trails as they move over the black racetrack.

9 When the race meet is over, remove the racers' numbers and put the snails back outside where you found them.

Helpful Earthworms

Earthworms are pinkish-gray, wriggly invertebrates that live in soil. Earthworms are very helpful to plants.

As earthworms burrow underground, they eat soil and dead plant matter, such as leaves, roots, and grass.

Inside their bodies, earthworms break down the plant matter they eat. Then they release it back into the soil as waste mixed in with soil. The broken-down plant matter in worm waste releases lots of good **nutrients** back into the soil. Plants can then feed on these nutrients.

As they burrow, earthworms also make the soil crumbly. This allows rainwater to trickle underground so that plants can suck it up through their roots.

soil

head

ringlike body sections called annuli (AN-yuh-ly)

Earthworm True and False

People sometimes say that if an earthworm is cut in two, each half will become a new worm. This is false! The half with the head may continue to live, but the tail half will be dead.

A heap of worm waste is called a worm casting.

Build a Worm Farm

You can watch **earthworms** at work in soil by building this worm farm!

You will need:

- Earthworms
- A small bowl
- Dead leaves and grass clippings
- An empty 2-liter soda bottle
- A knife (for an adult to use to cut the top off the bottle)
- A drill or ice pick (for adult use)
- Small stones or gravel
- Garden soil or potting compost
- Sand
- A large spoon
- ¾ cup (177 ml) of water
- Duct tape
- A plate
- An adult to be your teammate

Get Crafty:

1. Collect some earthworms by looking under large stones or pieces of dead wood. You can also dig in soil to find them. It's best to collect small worms as they need less space to live. Keep the worms cool and dark in a small bowl.

2. Collect some dead leaves and grass clippings, too, as worm food.

cut here

air holes

3 Ask an adult to cut the top off the soda bottle, about 2 inches (5 cm) from the top.

4 Now ask an adult to make six holes in the top section of the bottle to let in air, and six holes in the bottom to allow water to drain out. A drill or ice pick can be used to do this. Remove the cap of the bottle, too, to let in more air.

5 Place small stones, about 1 inch (2.5 cm) deep in the bottom of the bottle.

holes for water to drain

gravel

soil

sand

6 Place 1 inch (2.5 cm) of garden soil or potting compost on top of the stones. Then add 1 inch (2.5 cm) of sand on top of the soil. Keep repeating the layers of soil and sand until you are about an inch from the cut edge of the bottle.

7 Place some dead leaves and grass clippings on top of the soil. Add the worms on top of their food.

8 Ask an adult to tape the top section of the bottle to the bottom section using duct tape.

9 Place the worm farm in a cool, dark place because worms are most active at night. Stand the worm farm on a plate, which will catch any water that leaks out. After three days take a look. Is the food disappearing? Are the worms burrowing through the layers of sand and soil?

10 Add ¾ cup (177 ml) of water every three to four days, or if the soil looks dry. Add more food, too, as needed.

11 After two weeks, set your worms free where you found them.

Glossary

abdomen (AB-duh-mun)
The back section of an insect or spider's body. It contains the animal's heart and body parts for digesting food.

antennae (an-TEH-nee)
Long, thin body parts attached to the heads of insects. An insect's two antennae may be used for smelling and helping the insect balance.

arachnid (uh-RAK-nid)
An animal, such as a spider, scorpion, or tick, that has two main body parts and eight legs.

cephalothorax
(se-fuh-luh-THOR-aks)
The section of an arachnid's body that contains its mouth, eyes, and brain. The animal's legs are also attached to this section.

crops (KROPS)
Plants that are grown in large quantities on a farm.

exoskeleton (ek-soh-SKEH-leh-tun)
A hard outer covering on the body of an insect.

invertebrate (in-VER-teh-bret)
An animal without a backbone, such as an insect, worm, crab, or octopus.

mate (MAYT)
When a male and female come together to produce young.

nutrient (NOO-tree-ent)
A substance needed by plants or animals for health and growth.

palp (PALP)
A body part that looks like a short leg attached to the head of a spider. A spider's two palps are used for tasting food.

predator (PREH-duh-ter)
An animal that hunts and kills other animals for food.

prey (PRAY)
An animal that is hunted by another animal as food.

silk (SILK)
A shiny, soft, threadlike substance made in the bodies of spiders and some insects. People use silk to make fabric.

thorax (THOR-aks)
The chest section in the middle of an insect's body. An insect's six legs are attached to its thorax.

Websites

Due to the changing nature of Internet links, PowerKids Press has developed an online list of websites related to the subject of this book. This site is updated regularly. Please use this link to access the list:
www.powerkidslinks.com/gco/insect/

Read More

Burris, Judy, and Wayne Richards. *The Secret Lives of Backyard Bugs: Discover Amazing Butterflies, Moths, Spiders, Dragonflies, and Other Insects!*. North Adams, MA: Storey Publishing, 2011.

Marsh, Laura. *Spiders*. National Geographic Readers. Des Moines, IA: National Geographic Children's Books, 2012.

Rockwood, Leigh. *Worms are Gross!*. Creepy Crawlies. New York: PowerKids Press, 2011.

Index